D1133266

THE FOUR SEASONS

JAPANESE HAIKU
WRITTEN BY
BASHO · BUSON
ISSA · SHIKI · AND
MANY OTHERS

TRANSLATION BY
PETER BEILENSON

THE PETER
PAUPER PRESS
MOUNT VERNON · NEW YORK

THE FOUR SEASONS

DECORATIONS
BY MARIAN
MORTON

SPRING

SUCH A FINE FIRST DREAM...
  BUT THEY LAUGHED
  AT ME...THEY SAID
I HAD MADE IT UP
                    TAKUCHI

EVEN MY PLAIN WIFE...
  EXQUISITE AS VISITORS
ON NEW YEAR'S MORNING
                    ISO

NEW YEAR GIFT-GIVING...
  AH, BABY AT HER
  BARE BREAST
REACHING TINY HANDS
                    ISSA

FIRST WIND OF THE YEAR...
  THE OIL-LAMP
  IN THE WASHROOM
SHUDDERS AND IS STILL
                    OEMARU

6

FELICITATIONS!
 STILL...I GUESS
 THIS YEAR TOO
WILL PROVE ONLY SO-SO
                    ISSA

YEAR'S FIRST CART-LOAD...
 CUT-OUT PAPER
 FLOWERS DECK
THE EMACIATED HORSE
                    SHIKI

FIRST DREAM OF THE YEAR...
 I KEPT IT
 A DARK SECRET...
SMILING TO MYSELF
                    SHO-U

SUN-MELTED SNOW...
 WITH MY STICK
 I GUIDE THIS GREAT
DANGEROUS RIVER
                    ISSA

FROM MY TINY ROOF
　　SMOOTH ... SOFT ...
　　STILL-WHITE SNOW
MELTS IN MELODY

ISSA

ICICLES AND WATER
　　OLD DIFFERENCES
　　DISSOLVED ...
DRIP DOWN TOGETHER

TEISHITSU

OLD SNOW IS MELTING ...
　　NOW THE HUTS
　　UNFREEZING TOO
FREE ALL THE CHILDREN

ISSA

A CHILDLESS HOUSEWIFE ...
　　HOW TENDERLY
　　SHE TOUCHES
LITTLE DOLLS FOR SALE

RANSETSU

8

NOW WILD GEESE RETURN...
   WHAT DRAWS THEM
   CRYING CRYING
ALL THE LONG DARK NIGHT?
              ROKA

POURING FLOODS OF RAIN...
   WON'T MOUNT FUJI
   WASH AWAY
TO A MUDDY LAKE?
              BUSON

CLEAR-COLORED STONES
   ARE VIBRATING IN
   THE BROOK-BED...
OR THE WATER IS
              SOSEKI

IN MY NEW CLOTHING
   I FEEL SO DIFFERENT
   I MUST
LOOK LIKE SOMEONE ELSE
              BASHO

9

OH YOU BAWDY BREEZE . . .
   THATCHER BENDING
   ON THE ROOF
I SEE THE BOTTOM!

                ISSA

IMMOBILE FUJI . . .
   ALONE
   UNBLANKETED BY
MILLIONS OF NEW LEAVES

                BUSON

SPRING MORNING MARVEL . . .
   LOVELY NAMELESS
   LITTLE HILL
ON A SEA OF MIST

                BASHO

PASSING THE DOLL SHOP
   I PICKED UP
   THE LITTLEST ONE . . .
SUDDENLY I SMILED

                BAISHITSU

10

THERE IN THE WATER
COLOR OF THE
WATER MOVES . . .
TRANSLUCENT FISHES
                    RAIZAN

HAZY PONDED MOON
AND PALE NIGHT SKY
ARE BROKEN . . .
BUNGLING BLACK FROG
                    BUSON

SILVER-SOFT RIVERSIDE . . .
DIM SPLASH OF
FAR-THROWN NET . . .
FISHING FOR THE MOON?
                    TAIGI

PAPER-WEIGHTS PROTECT
GAY PICTURE-BOOKS
IN THE SHOP . . .
INQUISITIVE BREEZE
                    KITO

11

AH-AH-AH-CHOO! THAT
SPRING CATARRH!...
NOW I'VE LOST SIGHT
OF MY FIRST SKYLARK

YAYU

AN APRIL SHOWER...
SEE THAT THIRSTY
MOUSE LAPPING
RIVER SUMIDA

ISSA

RAINFALL IN APRIL...
TEARS FROM OUR
WEEPING WILLOW...
PETALS FROM OUR PLUM

SHOHA

AH LITTLE WARBLER...
THANKS-DROPPINGS
ON MY PORCH
BECAUSE I LOVE YOU?

BASHO

12

UNDER MY TREE-ROOF
   SLANTING LINES OF
   APRIL RAIN
SEPARATE TO DROPS
              BASHO

FARMER, RAISE YOUR HEAD...
   DIRECT THIS STRANGER
   WHO WILL SMILE
AND DISAPPEAR
              BUSON

GOOD MORNING, SPARROW...
   WRITING ON MY
   CLEAN VERANDA
WITH YOUR DEWY FEET
             SHIKI

BEACH FISHERMEN GO
   BOBBING OUT...
   BEACH POPPIES STAY
BENDING WITH SEA-BREEZE
             KYORAI

13

EVEN THE OCEAN
     RISING AND FALLING
     ALL DAY...
SIGHING GREEN LIKE TREES
                    BUSON

I COULD NOT SEE HIM
     THAT FLUTTERING
     FLY-OFF BIRD...
BUT THE PLUM-PETALS...
                    SHIKI

GLIDING RIVER BOAT...
     RISING SKYLARKS...
     RIPPLING SOUNDS
TO OUR RIGHT AND LEFT
                    RANKO

BIRD-DROPPINGS PATTERN
     THE PURPLES AND
     THE YELLOWS OF
MY IRIS PETALS
                    BUSON

SHINING ON THE SEA...
DAZZLING SUNLIGHT
SHAKING OVER
HILLS OF CHERRY-BLOOM

BUSON

OVER THE LOW HEDGE
HONEST PLUM
DISTRIBUTES PETALS
HALF INSIDE...HALF OUT

CHORA

RIVERBANK PLUM-TREE...
DO YOUR REFLECTED
BLOSSOMS
REALLY FLOW AWAY?

BUSON

BLUE EVENING SEA...
FROM SPRING ISLANDS
NEAR AND FAR
NEW LIGHTS ARE SHINING

SHIKI

THE OLD MESSENGER
   PROFFERING HIS
   PLUM-BRANCH FIRST...
ONLY THEN THE LETTER
KIKAKU

MIDNIGHT FULL OF STARS...
   DIM CHERRY-PETALS
   FLOATING ON
RICE-PADDY WATERS
BUSON

OVER MY SHOULDER...
   MY FRIENDS WHO
   FOLLOWED ME WERE LOST
IN CLOUDS OF BLOSSOM
CHORA

THE SEASHORE TEMPLE...
   INCOMING ROLLERS
   FLOW IN TIME
TO THE HOLY FLUTE
BUSON

LOW-TIDE MORNING...
   THE WILLOW'S SKIRTS
     ARE TRAILED
IN STINKING MUD

              BASHO

HERE COMES MR. HORSE...
   QUICK, QUICK, OUT
     OF THE ROADWAY
HAPPY SPARROWLET

              ISSA

MOONLIGHT STILLNESS
   LIGHTS THE PETALS
     FALLING...FALLING...
ON THE SILENCED LUTE

              SHIKI

GREEN...GREEN...GREEN...
   WILLOW-LEAF THREADS
     ARE SLIDING
RIVER-RUNNING-WATER

            ONITSURA

CHERRY-PETAL DAYS...
   BIRDS WITH TWO LEGS
   GLITTER NOW
HORSES GLEAM WITH FOUR
          ONITSURA

HEAT-WAVELETS RISING...
   PLUM-PETALS
   DRIFTING WAVERING
DOWN ON BURNING ROCKS
          SHIKI

COME NOW, PLAY WITH ME...
   FATHERLESS
   MOTHERLESS DEAR
LITTLE SPARROW-CHILD
          ISSA

NO BOLD RAIN-CLOUD FOR
   A HUNDRED MILES
   AROUND...DARES
BRAVE THE PEONIES
          BUSON

IN THE CLEAR FORDING
   PALE FEET OF THE
   SILENT GIRL ...
CLOUDING MAY WATERS
               BUSON

OPENING THIN ARMS ...
   A PINK PEONY
   BIG AS THIS!
SAID MY BITTY GIRL
               ISSA

ULTRA-PINK PEONY ...
   SILVER SIAMESE
   SOFT CAT ...
GOLD-DUST BUTTERFLY ...
               BUSON

ENERGETIC ANT ...
   SILHOUETTED ON
   THE STILL
SNOWFLAKE-PEONY
               BUSON

19

IN THE YARD PLUM-TREES
BLOSSOM . . . IN
THE BROTHEL
GIRLS ARE BUYING OBIS
BUSON

THAT WHITE PEONY . . .
LOVER OF THE MOON
TREMBLING
NOW AT TWILIGHT
GYODAI

FACING THE CANDLE
THE PEONY ALSO
BURNING . . .
MOTIONLESS AS DEATH
KYOROKU

THE FIRST FIREFLY . . .
BUT HE GOT AWAY
AND I . . .
AIR IN MY FINGERS
ISSA

LISTEN, ALL YOU FLEAS . . .
YOU CAN COME ON
PILGRIMAGE, O K . . .
BUT THEN, OFF YOU GIT!
ISSA

BUT IF I HELD IT . . .
COULD I TOUCH THE
LIGHTNESS OF THIS
FLUTTER-BUTTERFLY?
BUSON

HANGING SADLY DOWN
AMID THE
MERRY-MAKERS . . .
GREEN WEEPING WILLOW
ROKA SHONIN

OUT OF MY WAY PLEASE
AND LET ME PLANT
MY BAMBOOS . . .
OLD BROTHER TOAD
CHORA

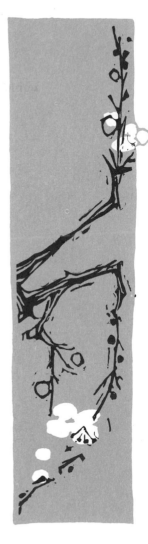

21

FOR THAT BRIEF MOMENT
   WHEN THE FIREFLY
   WENT OUT . . . O
THE LONELY DARKNESS
           HOKUSHI

NOW THIS OLD POET
   EMERGES FROM THE
   PURPLE DEPTHS
OF THE CONVOLVULUS
           CHORA

PINIONS PULSATING . . .
   YOUR MIND
   TRAVELING AFAR
BUTTERFLY DREAMER?
           CHIYO-NI

MOON-IN-THE-WATER . . .
   BROKEN-AGAIN . . .
   BROKEN-AGAIN . . .
STILL A SOLID SEAL
           CHOSU

NOW HAVING TAKEN
    WARMED WATER...
    THE VASE WELCOMES
MY CAMELLIA
                    ONITSURA

FALLEN NOW TO EARTH
    AFTER DANCING
    JOURNEYINGS...
KITE THAT LOST ITS SOUL
                    KUBONTA

KEEPING COMPANY
    WITH US, PIGEONS
    AND SPARROWS...
LOW-TIDE-LOOKERS ALL
                    ISSA

WHAT, TRAVELING
    IN THE RAIN?...
    BUT WHERE CAN HE
BE WENDING SNAILWARD?
                    ISSA

SUMMER

WITH MY NEW CLOTHING
ALAS ... SPRING
HAS BEEN BURIED
IN THAT WOODEN CHEST
SAIKAKU

HANDS UPON THE GROUND
OLD ARISTOCRATIC FROG
RECITES HIS POEM
SOKAN

AS I PICKED IT UP
TO CAGE IT ...
THE FIREFLY
LIT MY FINGER-TIPS
TAIGI

FLEEING THE HUNTER
THE FIREFLY
TOOK COVER ...
THE EVENING MOON
RYOTA

SOFTLY FOLDED FAWN
  SHIVERS, SHAKING OFF
  THE BUTTERFLY...
AND SLEEPS AGAIN

ISSA

THE HEAVY WAGON
  SHOOK ALL THE
  ROADSIDE...WAKING
A SINGLE BUTTERFLY

SHOHA

IN THE GOLDEN ROOM
  FRIGHTENED QUICK
  CALLIGRAPHY...
ESCAPING SWALLOW

BUSON

HE WADES THE RIVER
  CARRYING THE GIRL
  AND SEE...
CARRYING THE MOON

SHIKI

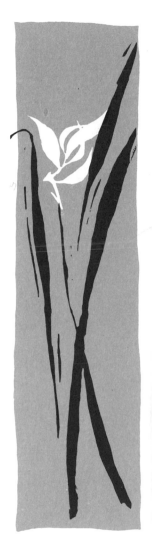

25

FOR DELICIOUSNESS
    TRY FORDING
    THIS RIVULET...
SANDALS IN ONE HAND

BUSON

ELEGANT SINGER
    WOULD YOU FURTHER
    FAVOR US
WITH A DANCE ... O FROG?

ISSA

BEFORE THE SACRED
    MOUNTAIN SHRINE
    OF KAMIJI...
MY HEAD BENT ITSELF

ISSA

RAINY AFTERNOON ...
    LITTLE DAUGHTER
    YOU WILL NEVER
TEACH THAT CAT TO DANCE

ISSA

ON THE LOW-TIDE BEACH
  EVERYTHING WE STOOP
  TO PICK ...
MOVES IN OUR FINGERS
                    CHIYO-NI

FLOWER-PETAL FELL ...
  THEN THE ROOSTER
  CROWED, AND SEE ...
ANOTHER PETAL
                    BAISHITSU

DARK THE WELL AT DAWN ...
  RISING WITH THE
  FIRST BUCKET ...
CAMELLIA-BLOSSOM
                    KAKEI

NOW TAKE THIS FLEA:
  HE SIMPLY CANNOT
  JUMP ... AND
I LOVE HIM FOR IT
                    ISSA

THE FLOATING HERON
    PECKS AT IT
    TILL IT SHATTERS ...
FULL-MOON-ON-WATER
                    ZUIRYU

FOR A COMPANION
    ON MY WALKING
    TRIP ... PERHAPS
A LITTLE BUTTERFLY
                    SHIKI

AH GOOD BUDDHIST FROG ...
    RISING TO A
    CLEARER LIGHT
BY NON-ATTACHMENT
                    JOSO

BATS COME OUT AT DUSK ...
    WOMAN OVER
    THE WAY ... WHY
DO YOU STARE AT ME?
                    BUSON

OVERHANGING PINE...
   ADDING ITS MITE
   OF NEEDLES
TO THE WATERFALL
BASHO

SQUADS OF FROGS JUMPED IN
   WHEN THEY HEARD
   THE PLUNK-PLASH
OF A SINGLE FROG
WAKYU

LITTLE SILVER FISH
   POINTING UPSTREAM
   MOVING DOWNSTREAM
IN CLEAR QUICK WATER
SOSEKI

LOOK...THE PALACE...
   YOU CAN GLIMPSE IT
   THROUGH THAT HOLE
IN THE MOSQUITO-FOG
ISSA

CONGRATULATIONS
   ISSA!...YOU HAVE
   SURVIVED TO FEED
THIS YEAR'S MOSQUITOES
              ISSA

IN YOUR SUMMER-ROOM...
   GARDEN AND MOUNTAIN
   GOING TOO
AS WE SLOWLY WALK
              BASHO

JUST BEYOND THE SMOKE
   OF OUR SMUDGE
   THIS EVENING...
MOSQUITO-MUSIC
              SHIRAO

DO I HEAR VOICES
   FROM FAR LANDS
   ABOVE THE CLOUDS?
O...SILLY SKYLARKS
              KYOROKU

SHORTEST SUMMER NIGHT...
   IN EARLY MORNING
   LAMPS STILL
BURNING ON THE BAY
             SHIKI

MOON-IN-THE-WATER
   TURNED A WHITE
   SOMERSAULT...YES
AND WENT FLOATING OFF
             RYOTA

EVEN FLY-SWATTING
   BY THESE BORDER
   GUARDS ... O HOW
VICIOUS AND CORRECT
             TAIGI

QUICK-PATTERING RAIN ...
   CHANCE AND VANITY
   DICTATE
GAY IMPROMPTU HATS
             OTSUYU

YOU HEAR THAT FAT FROG
   IN THE SEAT OF
   HONOR, SINGING
BASS?...THAT'S THE BOSS
               ISSA

WINDY-WEB SPIDER
   WHAT IS YOUR
   SILENT SPEAKING...
YOUR UNSUNG SONG?
              BASHO

AND EACH MORNING
   RIGHT ABOVE THIS
   LITTLE ROOF...
MY PRIVATE SKYLARK
              JOSO

DON'T WASTE PRECIOUS TIME
   NOW, TAGGING ALONG
   WITH ME...
BROTHER BUTTERFLY
              ISSA

EXPERIMENTING . . .
  I HUNG THE MOON
  ON VARIOUS
BRANCHES OF THE PINE
HOKUSHI

SWAT SOFTLY SOFTLY
  AT THE SICK-ROOM
  FLIES . . . BECAUSE
I SEEK FOR SLEEP
SHIKI

THE DEVOTED CLERK . . .
  NOT TO WASTE
  A JOT OF BREEZE
NAPS ON A LEDGER PILLOW
ISSA

ON HIS GARDEN PATH
  THIS SPARROW
  SCATTERS PEBBLES . . .
MAN FORGOTTEN
SHOHA

RIVER MOGAMI
  WINDING FROM
    NORTHERN MOUNTAINS
WASHES WARM SUMMER
SHIKI

SUMMER-NIGHT INSECTS
  FALLING BURNT AND
    DEAD ... UPON
MY POEM'S PAPER
SHIKI

YOU ARE JUST TOO LATE
  TO HELP ME WITH
    THE LAMP ... MY MOTH
LIGHT-EXTINGUISHER
ISSA

AGAIN COOLNESS COMES ...
  SILVER UNDERSIDES
    OF LEAVES
EVENING-BREEZE BLOWN
SHIKI

AFTER THAT ILLNESS
   MY LONG GAZING
   AT ROSES
WEARIED THE EYELIDS
SHIKI

THE NIGHT WAS HOT...
   STRIPPED TO THE WAIST
   THE SNAIL
ENJOYED THE MOONLIGHT
ISSA

MY SUMMER ILLNESS...
   BUT AT LAST MY LIFE
   WAS SPARED
AT THE VERY BONES
SHIKI

CAREFUL, CHAMPION FLEA
   AND LOOK BEFORE
   YOU LEAP...
HERE'S RIVER SUMIDA
ISSA

COMING FROM THE BATH...
   COOL ON HER BREASTS
     THE WARM BREEZE
OF THE VERANDA

             SHIKI

FUI! A SOUR PLUM...
   THIN EYEBROWS
     PINCHED TOGETHER
ON THE LOVELY FACE

             BUSON

HOLY NOON DUET:
   BASSO-SNORING
     PRIEST...DEVOUT
CONTRALTO-CUCKOO

             SHIKI

FARTHER IN THE GROVE
   THE LANTERN WALKS...
     NEARER NEARER
SINGS THE NIGHTINGALE

             SHIKI

WITH THE NEW CLOTHES
   REMEMBER . . . THE
   CROW STAYS BLACK
AND THE HERON WHITE
               CHORA

I SCOOPED UP THE MOON
   IN MY WATER
   BUCKET . . . AND
SPILLED IT ON THE GRASS
              RYUHO

MUST YOU COME TO VEX
   MY SICK EYES THAT
   STILL CAN MOVE . . .
BED-CRISS-CROSSING FLY?
              SHIKI

COOLNESS ON THE BRIDGE . . .
   MOON, YOU AND I
   ALONE
UNRESIGNED TO SLEEP
           KIKUSHA-NI

IN THE ENDLESS RAIN
 IS IT TURNING
 SUNWARD STILL ...
TRUSTING HOLLYHOCK?
BASHO

HOT SLOW AFTERNOON ...
 SUDDENLY THE HAND
 HAS STOPPED ...
SLOW-FALLING FAN
TAIGI

IN SUMMER MOONLIGHT
 THEY GO VISITING
 THE GRAVES ...
SAVORING THE COOL
ISSA

IN THE MORNING BREEZES
 CLIMBING IN A
 SINGLE LINE
GO SINGING SKYLARKS
RYOTA

A NEAR NIGHTINGALE . . .
   BUT MY HEAD JUST
   COULDN'T FIT
THROUGH THE LATTICES
             YAHA

A SUMMER SHOWER . . .
   ALONG ALL THE
   STREET, SERVANTS
SLAPPING SHUT SHUTTERS
             SHIKI

RAINFALL AND THUNDER
   BEATING ON BOARDS
   AND BLOSSOMS . . .
INDISCRIMINATE
             SAMPO

RAIN-OBLITERATED . . .
   THE RIVER,
   SOME ROOFS,
A BRIDGE WITHOUT A SHORE
             BASHO

AUTUMN

IN LANTERN-LIGHT
   MY YELLOW
   CHRYSANTHEMUMS
LOST ALL THEIR COLOR

BUSON

MORNING-MISTED STREET...
   WITH WHITE INK
   AN ARTIST BRUSHES
A DREAM OF PEOPLE

BUSON

AT NARA TEMPLE...
   FRESH-SCENTED
   CHRYSANTHEMUMS
AND ANCIENT IMAGES

BASHO

AN OLD TREE WAS FELLED...
   ECHOING, DARK ECHOING
THUNDER IN THE HILLS

MEISETSU

THE GREAT FIRE OF KANDA

HEAT-WAVES TO HEAVEN . . .
 RISING FROM THE
 RUINED HEARTS OF
THREE THOUSAND HOMES
                    SHIKI

CHANTING AT THE ALTAR
 OF THE INNER
 SANCTUARY . . .
A CRICKET PRIEST
                    ISSA

SAD TWILIGHT CRICKET . . .
 YES, I HAVE WASTED
 ONCE AGAIN
THOSE DAYLIGHT HOURS
                    RIKEI

A SUDDEN SHOWER . . .
 TERRIFIED, LOUD
 IDIOT DUCKS
HIGH-TAILING HOME
                    KIKAKU

41

MY MELONS THAT YOU
   STOLE LAST YEAR ...
  THIS YEAR I PLACE
UPON YOUR GRAVE, MY SON
OEMARU

ON THESE RAINY DAYS
   THAT OLD POET
   RYOKAN
WALLOWS IN SELF-PITY
RYOKAN

PITIFUL ... FEARFUL ...
   THESE POOR SCARECROWS
   LOOK LIKE MEN
IN AUTUMN MOONLIGHT
SHIKI

WE STAND STILL TO HEAR
   TINKLE OF FAR
   TEMPLE BELL ...
WILLOW-LEAVES FALLING
BASHO

THE EVENING BREEZES ...
   WATER LAPPING
   LIGHTLY ON
THE HERON'S LEG-STICKS
               BUSON

THE WET KINGFISHER
   SHAKES HIS FEATHERS
   IN THE LATE
REFLECTED SUNLIGHT
              TORI

IN UNENDING RAIN
   THE HOUSE-PENT BOY
   IS FRETTING
WITH HIS BRAND-NEW KITE
             SHOHA

THE CALLING BELL
   TRAVELS THE CURLING
   MIST-WAYS ...
AUTUMN MORNING
           BASHO

NIGHTLONG IN THE COLD
   THAT MONKEY SITS
   CONJECTURING
HOW TO CATCH THE MOON
           SHIKI

DARK UNENDING NIGHT...
   ONCE, OUTSIDE
   THE PAPER SCREEN,
A LANTERN PASSING
           SHIKI

THEY HAVE GONE ... BUT
   THEY LIT THE
   GARDEN LANTERN
OF THEIR LITTLE HOUSE
           SHIKI

ON ONE RIVERBANK
   SUNBEAMS SLANTING
   DOWN ... BUT ON
THE OTHER ... RAINDROPS
           BUSON

44

SUPPER IN AUTUMN...
   FLAT LIGHT THROUGH
   AN OPEN DOOR
FROM A SETTING SUN
CHORA

SEPTEMBER SUNSHINE...
   THE HOVERING
   DRAGONFLY'S
SHIMMERING SHADOW
KARO

DO I DARE DEPEND
   UPON YOU FOR
   FIRM FRIENDSHIP
DEAR MORNING-GLORY?
BASHO

A WINDBLOWN GRASS...
   HOVERING MID-AIR
   IN VAIN
AN AUTUMN DRAGONFLY
BASHO

NOW THE OLD SCARECROW
  LOOKS JUST LIKE
  OTHER PEOPLE...
DRENCHING AUTUMN RAIN
         SEIBI

HERE IS THE DARK TREE
  DENUDED NOW
  OF LEAFAGE...
BUT A MILLION STARS
         SHIKI

UP FROM MY ILLNESS
  I WENT TO THE
  CHRYSANTHEMUMS...
HOW COLD THEY SMELLED!
         OTSUJI

WAKING IN THE NIGHT
  I ADDED MY AUTUMN
  COUGHING
TO INSECT VOICES
         JOSO

JAGGED CANDLE-FLAME...
THE VERY SHAPE
OF AUTUMN SIFTS
THROUGH THE SHUTTERS
RAIZAN

URGING ON MY HORSE
INTO MIST-BLANKETED
WATER...
RIVER-GURGLE SOUNDS
TAIGI

WHITE CHRYSANTHEMUMS
MAKING ALL ELSE
ABOUT THEM
REFLECTED RICHES
CHORA

PEACEFULNESS...TODAY
FUJIAMA STANDS
ABOVE US
MIST-INVISIBLE
BASHO

SMACK-ACK...SMACK-ACK...
   MEN DRIVING
   FISH-NET STAKES
IN WHITE-FOG MORNING
                  BUSON

WHITE AUTUMN MOON...
   BLACK-BRANCH
   SHADOW-PATTERNS
PRINTED ON THE MATS
                  KIKAKU

EXQUISITE THE DEWY
   BRAMBLE...
   TO EVERY THORN
A SINGLE DROPLET
                  BUSON

FROM THE TEMPLE STEPS
   I LIFT TO THE
   AUTUMN MOON
MY VERITABLE FACE
                  BASHO

IN THIS SOLID MIST
    WHAT ARE THOSE
    PEOPLE SHOUTING
BETWEEN BOAT AND HILL?
KITO

NIGHTS ARE GETTING COLD . . .
    NOT A SINGLE INSECT
    NOW
ATTACKS THE CANDLE
SHIKI

HIS HAT BLOWN OFF . . .
    HOW PITILESS
    THE PELTING
STORM ON THE SCARECROW
HAGI-JO

IN MY OWN VILLAGE
    I THINK THERE ARE
    MORE SCARECROWS LEFT
THAN OTHER PEOPLE
CHASEI

SWALLOWS FLYING SOUTH . . .
  MY HOUSE TOO
  OF STICKS AND PAPER
ONLY A STOPPING-PLACE
              KYORAI

AFTER MOON-VIEWING
  MY COMPANIONABLE
  SHADOW
WALKED ALONG WITH ME
               SODO

AFTER THE WINDSTORM
  FORAGING FOR
  FIREWOOD . . .
THREE FIERCE OLD WOMEN
              BUSON

ROADSIDE BARLEY-STALKS
  TORN BY OUR CLUTCHING
  FINGERS . . .
AS WE SMILED FAREWELL
              BASHO

SUDDENLY CHILL FALL ...
  WHY SHOULD THAT
  RAGGED FORTUNE-TELLER
LOOK SO SURPRISED?

BUSON

ALL THE WORLD IS COLD ...
  MY FISHING-LINE
  IS TREMBLING
IN THE AUTUMN WIND

BUSON

AUTUMN BREEZES SHAKE
  THE SCARLET FLOWERS
  MY POOR CHILD
COULD NOT WAIT TO PICK

ISSA

SEEKING IN MY HUT
  FOR UNLOCKED
  MIDNIGHT TREASURES ...
A CRICKET BURGLAR

ISSA

51

WINTER

LITTLE ORPHAN GIRL...
   EATING A LONELY DINNER
IN WINTER TWILIGHT
          SHOHAKU

IN THE WINTRY MOON
   GALES RAGING
   DOWN THE RIVER
HONE THE ROCK-EDGES
          CHORA

THE NEW-LAID GARDEN...
   ROCKS SETTLING
   IN HARMONY
IN SOFT WINTER RAIN
          SHADO

WHEN I RAISED MY HEAD...
   THERE WAS MY
   RIGID BODY
LYING BITTER COLD
          SEIBI

OVER WINTRY FIELDS
   BOLD SPARROW
   COMPANIES FLY
SCARECROW TO SCARECROW
            SAZANAMI

BATH-TUB FIREWOOD...
   THANKS FOR THIS
   FINAL SERVICE
FAITHFUL OLD SCARECROW
            JOSO

MY VERY BONE-ENDS
   MADE CONTACT WITH
   THE ICY QUILTS
OF DEEP DECEMBER
            BUSON

POOR THIN CRESCENT
   SHIVERING AND
   TWISTED HIGH...
IN THE BITTER DARK
            ISSA

SO LONELY...LOVELY...
   THE EXQUISITE
    PURE-WHITE FAN
OF THE GIRL I LOST

          BUSON

IN WINTER MOONLIGHT
   A CLEAR LOOK
    AT MY OLD HUT...
DILAPIDATED

          ISSA

BLACK CALLIGRAPHY
   OF GEESE...PALE
    PRINTED FOOTHILLS...
FOR A SEAL, FULL MOON

          BUSON

IN MY DARK WINTER
   LYING ILL...
    AT LAST I ASK
HOW FARES MY NEIGHBOR?

          BASHO

THE OLD DOG LIES INTENT
    LISTENING ...
    DOES HE OVERHEAR
THE BURROWING MOLES?
                    ISSA

A THOUSAND ROOF-TOPS
    A THOUSAND
    MARKET-VOICES ...
WINTER-MORNING MIST
                    BUSON

FIRST SNOW LAST NIGHT ...
    THERE ACROSS THE
    MORNING BAY
SUDDEN MOUNTAIN-WHITE
                    SHIKI

WHEN THE WATERPOT
    BURST THAT SILENT
    NIGHT WITH COLD ...
MY EYES SPLIT OPEN
                    BASHO

WINTER HAVING TOUCHED
THESE FIELDS . . .
THE VERY TOMTITS
PERCH ON THE SCARECROW
KIKAKU

COLD WINTER RAINFALL . . .
MINGLING ALL THEIR
GLEAMING HORNS
OXEN AT THE FENCE
RANKO

SEE THE RED BERRIES . . .
FALLEN LIKE LITTLE
FOOTPRINTS
ON THE GARDEN SNOW
SHIKI

WINTER-EVENING SNOW . . .
THE UNCOMPLETED
BRIDGE IS ALL
AN ARCH OF WHITENESS
BASHO

MOONLIT SNOWFIELDS . . .
   HERE THE BLOODIED
   SAMURAI
CAST THEIR NOBLE LIVES
            KIKAKU

MIDNIGHT WANDERER
   WALKING THROUGH
   THE SNOWY STREET . . .
ECHOING DOG-BARK
          SHIKI

AS TO ICICLES
   I OFTEN WONDER
   WHY THEY GROW
SOME LONG . . . SOME SHORT
         ONITSURA

IN WINTER MOONLIGHT
   FISH-NET STAKES
   CAST THEIR SHIFTING
UNEVEN SHADOWS
        SHIRAO

COLDER FAR THAN SNOW...
   WINTER MOONLIGHT
   ECHOING ON
MY WHITENED HAIR

               JOSO

SO CLOSE ... SO VAST ...
   RATTLING WINTER
   HAILSTONES ON
MY UMBRELLA-HAT

              BASHO

LONG-WALKING LANTERN
   DISAPPEARED INTO
   SOME HOUSE ...
DESOLATE WHITE HILLS

              SHIKI

SOLITARY CROW ...
   COMPANIONING
   MY PROGRESS
OVER SNOWY FIELDS

              SENNA

STARING DELIGHTED
    EVEN AT WALKING
    HORSES
IN NEW MORNING SNOW
                    BASHO

BLINDING WILD SNOW
    BLOWS, WHIRLS AND
    DRIFTS ABOUT ME . . .
IN THIS WORLD ALONE
                    CHORA

WINTER MOONLIGHT CASTS
    COLD TREE-SHADOWS
    LONG AND STILL . . .
MY WARM ONE MOVING
                    SHIKI

IN THAT COLD DARKNESS
    MY HORSE STUMBLED
    SUDDENLY
JUST OUTSIDE THE HOUSE
                    BUSON

LOOK AT THAT STRAY CAT
   SLEEPING . . . SNUG
   UNDER THE EAVES
IN THE WHISTLING SNOW

        TAIGI

IN MY NEW-YEAR HEART
   I FEEL NO FURY . . .
   EVEN AT
THESE TRAMPLERS OF SNOW

        YAYU

COFFIN AND MOURNERS
   PASSED ME WALKING
   DOWN THE STREET . . .
MIDNIGHT AT NEW YEAR'S

        SHIKI

TO CELEBRATE NEW YEAR'S
   WE FEAST
   NEWLY-OPENED EYES ON
SNOWY FUJIAMA

        SOKAN

DEATH-SONG:

POET NIGHTINGALE . . .
   WILL I HEAR YOUR
   LATER VERSES
IN THE VALE OF DEATH?

ANON.

DEATH-SONG:

SUDDENLY YOU LIGHT
   AND AS SUDDENLY
   GO DARK . . .
FELLOW-FIREFLY

CHINE-JO

DEATH-SONG:

FULL-MOON AND FLOWERS
   SOLACING MY FORTY-NINE
FOOLISH YEARS OF SONG

ISSA

DEATH-SONG:

IF THEY ASK FOR ME
   SAY: HE HAD SOME
   BUSINESS
IN ANOTHER WORLD

SOKAN